RYAN'S BIG CHOICE
TO PICK HIS INNER VOICE

Ryan's Big Choice To Pick His Inner Voice

Tonya T. Rice

Path To Purpose Publishing, LLC

Ryan and his friend, Tiana, were on their way home from school. "Hey Ryan! Guess what? I got an "A" on my math test!" said Tiana excitedly.

Ryan frowned. "It must be nice to be smart, instead of being stupid like me."

"You're not stupid," said Tiana.

"Yes, I am!

"No, you aren't!"

"Yes, I am! I have proof!" Ryan answered.

"What's your proof?" Tiana asked.

Ryan explained that when he was taking a test, other kids finished before he was done.

"See! This proves that I am stupid."

"Who told you that?" Tiana asked.

Ryan and Tiana heard a voice yell out, "I know!"

Just then, an angel CLIMBED OUT OF RYAN'S EAR and sat on his shoulder.

"You don't know anything!" said another voice coming from Ryan's other ear.

"Who are you guys?" Ryan asked.

"My name is Angelo!" said the angel. It's nice to be here with you!"

"It is your greatest honor to meet me! I am the dashing, daring, and dynamic Devlin!"

Just then an angel popped out of Tiana's ear.
"Hi! I am Angela! Angelo and I work to give you wise advice to help you have a good life," she said.
"Make way for the dazzling, dramatic diva!" said Devila, who appeared on Tiana's shoulder. "I am here to make sure that Tiana has an...eventful life."

Devlin looked at Ryan and said, "I am the MOST IMPORTANT voice in your head, kid!"

"Devlin is the one who told you that you are stupid," explained Angelo.

"Of course, I did! He was the last kid done with his test! Everyone was waiting for him to finish. He probably got all the answers wrong too!"said Devlin.

"Probably!" laughed Devila.

"Don't listen to them, Ryan. Devlin and Devila lie and say mean things to make you feel bad. They tell you to do things that are not good for you to get you hurt or in trouble," explained Angelo.

"Shut up Angelo! No one asked you!" yelled Devlin. "I just tell the kid the truth, even if it hurts his little feelings."

"You don't tell the truth! You lie all the time," said Angelo.

Devlin smiled slyly. "I'm here to look out for the kid's best interests."

"Really? What about the time when Ryan's mother told him not to touch the hot stove?"

Devlin started to laugh, "*Ha ha ha*! I remember that! I told the kid to do whatever he wants to do and not let his mom ruin his life with her rules."

And I told him to listen to his mother," said Angelo.

"Exactly!" exclaimed Devlin, "You are so boring! Let the kid have some fun!"

"So, Ryan listened to you and touched the hot stove. He burned his hand and was in so much pain! I was so sad for him. What did you say to Ryan after he got burned?" asked Angelo.

"I told him he was stupid for touching the stove and he deserved to get burned!" replied Devlin.

Angelo turned to Ryan and explained that it is the angel's job to tell the truth and to protect, help and calm people. "We want you to feel proud, confident and happy in life. We don't want you to be hurt or afraid."

Devlin rolled his eyes, "Blah, blah, blah! Don't listen to him! With me, you will get the cold, hard truth! Someone has to let you know all the bad things about you and everyone else. We tell you when to feel afraid, guilty or embarrassed. We give you lots of reasons for why we are right, and those annoying angels are wrong."

"Just like in class!" Devlin continued, "I told you that smart kids finish first. You are slow. Being slow is bad. Schoolwork is easy for smart kids. So, if it's not easy for you, then you MUST be stupid!"

That's a lie!" exclaimed Angelo. "Ryan, you just need to do your best. It's smart to take your time and ask for help when you need it. You are smart!"

Ryan was confused, "I don't know who to believe!"
"Listen to your heart, Ryan. If you feel calm and peaceful when you get a thought, then trust that. If it feels bad or wrong, then it is bad and wrong," Angela replied.

"You need to believe me kid! I am ALWAYS right!" exclaimed Devlin. "Believe the voice in your head that's the loudest and talks the most!"
Devila agreed, "Yeah! Believe the voice in your head that makes you worried! Fear keeps you on your toes. It tells you everything that could ever go wrong so that you can plan for it".

Angelo shook his head in disagreement, "Fear makes you worry about things that have not happened, and probably will not happen, just to make you feel bad." Devlin and Devila began snickering and whispering to each other. "It's funny when they feel bad!"

We have to go now. Goodbye Tiana! Good-bye Ryan!" Angela said.

Angelo waved goodbye and said,

"Ryan, you are an incredible boy and I am glad I get to be in your mind with you."

Devlin yelled out, "See ya suckers!"

"See ya, wouldn't want to be ya!" Devila said before all four of them disappeared.

Whoa! That was crazy!" said Ryan

Tiana agreed and then she asked Ryan, "So...which one of them do you believe?"

Ryan thought for a while then he replied, "I think that the angels tells the truth and the devils lie..."

Tiana then asked, "So, do you still think you are stupid?"
Ryan thought longer and then said, "If Angelo tells me the truth and Devlin tells me lies, I guess that means that I'm not stupid after all!"

Tonya T. Rice is an author and Licensed Professional Counselor (LPC) in the state of Michigan and is a board certified National Certified Counselor (NCC).
She has extensive experience counseling and educating people in
the field of mental health. She is a wife and mother of three wonderful children and two adorable Yorkie dogs.

Isabella Wilson is a talented artist and illustrator. She has extensive experience with a variety of art styles that include, digital art, sketching, painting, clay, and pointillism. She has earned several awards for her artwork, which has been featured in several art shows in Michigan. She plans to continue her career in art, animation and film directing. She enjoys spending time with her friends and camping with her family.

CPSIA information can be obtained
at www.ICGtesting.com
Printed in the USA
LVHW070143141120
671609LV00014B/525